T0368076

# MALAWI ASSEMBLIES OF GOD: CHURCH PLANTING AND DISCIPLESHIP

Published by
Luviri Press
P/Bag 201, Luwinga, Mzuzu

ISBN 978-99960-968-6-0

A Luviri Text

Cover design: Josephine Kawejere

Printed by Lightening Source

# CHURCH PLANTING AND DISCIPLESHIP: UNLOCKING THE FEASIBLE GROWTH

## LAWRENCE CHIPAO

LUVIRI PRESS

MZUZU

2016

# CONTENTS

# PART A: Church Planting

## INTRODUCTION

Malawi Assemblies of God church embarked on a feasible journey of **Vision 2020** that included every established church to plant one church and send one student to Bible school each year. From the time this vision was adopted, some churches have responded positively and some are still struggling on where and how to get involved. We realize that there are big challenges to most of the churches in the organization. Some churches feel they are too small for the heavy responsibility. But we all start with small things, in other ways from a position where we can manage. Every church in the Malawi Assemblies of God has the potential and can participate in the agreement. The call to all of its members is "LET'S DO IT." It is doable.

This booklet is a church planting and growth manual that will assist those that feel it is too difficult to plant and raise a church and those who would like to add knowledge in their task. Remember, we are not just planting, but we are caring to make sure that the church planted is a growing congregation and will be there till rapture time. Discipleship will be emphasized in this manual. Discipleship is considered as the missing link in the church planting effort.

# 1) IMPORTANCE OF CHURCH PLANTING

## 1. JESUS TOLD US TO DO IT

i) **John 20:21** Upper room in Jerusalem after the Resurrection to 10 disciples - I am sending you (**Commission**).

ii) **Mark 16:15** Upper room in Jerusalem a week later to 11 disciples - Go to the entire world and preach to every person (**Recipients**).

iii) **Matt. 28:19, 20** Mountain in Galilee, at least two weeks later to 11 disciples - Disciple all "peoples" then baptize and teach (**Strategy**).

iv) **Luke 24:46-48** Jerusalem on the 40th day to 11 disciples - Preach repentance and forgiveness of sins based on the resurrection of Christ (**Content**).

v) **Acts 1:8** on Mt. of Olive, on the 40th day to 11 disciples - Jerusalem to the uttermost parts of the earth (**Geography**).

## 2. THE EARLY CHURCH SET THE PRECEDENT

Throughout the book of Acts, we see that whenever the disciples went about fulfilling the Great Commission, they planted churches.

## 3. HISTORY SHOWS THAT CHURCH PLANTING AND REVIVAL WERE LINKED

i) The New Testament Church is the first example.

ii) History tells us that each of the apostles were involved in church planting in various countries.

iii) John Wesley is by far the most remembered because he used the strategy of church planting which resulted in the Methodist Movement.

## 4. RESEARCH SHOWS THAT CHURCH PLANTING IS THE MOST EFFECTIVE AND EFFICIENT MEANS OF EVANGELISM

i) Dr. Peter Wagner states: "The single most effective evangelistic methodology under Heaven is planting new churches."

ii) Major Pentecostal and Evangelical denominations across the world have formulated detailed strategies for church planting because they have realized the interrelation between church planting and evangelization.

# 5. CHURCH PLANTING BUILDS A NETWORK THAT CAPTURES THE HARVEST

i) One church in a community is not enough to capture the harvest. The effective Mega-churches are rare.

ii) Having an entire network of new churches increases the effectiveness of the gospel in the community.

    a. Fishing with a line will catch fish.

    b. Fishing with two lines will catch more fish.

    c. Fishing with a net catches a lot more fish.

iii) **Consequently, we ought to view multiple church planting as building a network that captures God's harvest.**

# 6. NEW CHURCHES ARE FRESH, POSITIVE AND HUNGRY FOR GROWTH

i) So many established churches have settled down into what they consider to be comfortable, so that the effort to reach out to new people slows down dramatically.

ii) New churches are much more zealous for souls, for growth, for the integration of new people.

# 7. NEW CHURCHES RELEASE MORE PEOPLE INTO EFFECTIVE MINISTRY (NEW CONGREGATIONS ARE MORE EVANGELISTIC)

i) Many gifted people are sitting in established older churches not fully utilizing their spiritual gifts.

ii) New churches tend to release more people into utilizing their spiritual gifts, which results in a more effective witness in the community.

# 8. CHURCH PLANTING IS THE MOST EFFECTIVE METHOD IN THE TASK OF REACHING THE WORLD

i) The world's population is growing at a tremendous rate.

ii) Adding people to churches will not keep up with the growth rate.

iii) The only way to effectively evangelize and establish disciples is through church planting multiplication.

## 9. CHURCH PLANTING STIMULATES EXISTING CHURCHES

i) The best thing that can happen to an old established church, at times, is for a new church to be planted nearby. It becomes a reminder that we need to be constantly addressing our goals and cannot afford to become complacent or lazy.

ii) New churches also add to the spiritual awareness of a community and everyone benefits as a result.

## 11. NEW CHURCHES ARE THE MAIN KEY TO DENOMINATIONAL GROWTH

It is a fact that no-one can deny. Denominations that fail to plant churches are decreasing in membership. Lyle Schaller reports that every denomination that records an increase in membership also reports an increase in the number of congregations. Conversely, every denomination that records a decrease in membership also reports a decrease in congregations.

## 12. OUR GOAL IS TO SEE 'THE WHOLE WORLD FILLED WITH HIS GLORY'— CHURCH PLANTING IS GOD'S KEY TO SEEING THIS COME TO PASS

Jesus said in Matt 16:18b, "I will build my church and the gates of Hades shall not prevail against it." The picture Jesus gives us is a strong progressive visionary church that is plundering hell and populating Heaven. A church that is unstoppable by any force of any enemy.

NOTE: Church planting is not an option—it is a priority. We can never afford to sit back and be glad of what we already have, when there is still so much ground to capture.

## 2) PROFILE OF A CHURCH PLANTER

1. A DEFINITE CALL OF GOD

Good ideas do not build strong churches. God's ideas do. A church planter needs to hear the Great Commission from the Great Commissioner and know without a doubt that he/she has been sent out to do the great task of church planting.

2. SPIRITUAL QUALITIES

   i)    A Person of Prayer.
   ii)   A Person full of the Holy Spirit.
   iii)  A Person that demonstrates the fruit of the Spirit.
   iv)   Sound Bible knowledge.
   v)    The qualities listed in 1 Timothy 3:1-7.

3. THE SPIRITUAL GIFTS

Church growth should never become so mechanical and scientific that it removes God from the equation. He is the Great Commissioner (Matt 28:18-20), the Gift Giver (1 Cor 12:4-6), the Giver of the Holy Spirit (Lk 24:49).

4. THE NATURAL SKILLS

Natural skills are those skills that diligent people pick up by:
   i)    Reading books
   ii)   Attending courses
   iii)  Observing and analyzing the experiences of others
   iv)   Learning from one's own life experiences, both positive and negative.

Some of the natural skills needed by a church planter are:
   i)    To be a Visionary
   ii)   To be a People Person
   iii)  To be a Communicator

**NOTE:**

A visionary church planter, who is a people person and is able to communicate and motivate people to follow Jesus, will never preach to empty seats. There will always be a crowd who will come and hear the message from this person.

## 3) THE ROLE OF A CHURCH PLANTER

- His/her authority in the church as God's leader is a moral and spiritual power, not a legal one.

- He/she should exercise leadership.

- He/she must refuse to compromise biblical convictions, even though they should be gracious in attitude, and never be stubborn about personal opinions or desires that do not involve biblical principles.

- His/her authority rests in the power of a godly example, as well as in the fact that they are a biblical officer (1 Pet. 5:3, Eph. 4:11, 12). However, he is not to be a "lord over God's heritage" (1 Pet. 5:1-4). He has no biblical right to be autocratic, dictatorial or domineering. No man or woman of God, filled with the Spirit, will manifest such an attitude.

**NOTE:**
The church must allow its leaders to lead. The pastorate is a leading office. This does not mean dictatorship, control or even ownership of the property. If the people do not follow, then the failure is with the leader. The deacons' committee must give wisdom and guidance to the pastor and to the congregation. They are a serving office while they work behind the scene; they must work together with pastors and people (1 Cor. 3:9).

# 4) IMPORTANT ELEMENTS FOR CHURCH PLANTING INITIATIVES

1. **Prayer:** Prayer is the starting point for all ministry. Know the mind of God and join Him in His work.

2. **Scripture:** Scripture is foundational and the source of all teaching and preaching. Scripture → Principle → Practice

3. **Disciples:** Make Disciples, not converts. Converts focus on religion. Disciples focus on Jesus and obedience to His teachings.

4. **Obedience:** Teach Obedience to the Word, not doctrine. Doctrine is our church's teaching from the Bible. It may be highly interpretive, and may not consider the full counsel of the Bible.

5. **Communities of Believers (Church):** Form new believers into minimum Biblical practice groups that will become Communities of Believers (churches) who transform families and communities

6. **Authority and the Holy Spirit:** Authority of Scripture and the Holy Spirit are all that is needed to start. Church Planting is an act of God through His Spirit and His people who are obedient to the Word and the Spirit.

7. **Spiritual Warfare:** In areas where the Gospel has never been preached, or in areas where traditional religions have reigned for a significant amount of time, it is not unusual to find those engaging in Church Planting activities confronted by Spiritual Conflicts that range from annoying to life-threatening.

8. **Home cells/groups:** Groups/Communities learn more quickly, remember more things and better replicate more quickly and often when correctly led, protected against heresy, and protected against bad leadership.

9. **Plan/Be Intentional:** Plan your work and work your plan. Be intentional in Access Ministry, Prayer, Scripture, Appropriate Evangelism and Church Planting.

10. **Access Ministries:** Access Ministries open the door for Church Planting and lead to community transformation. Ministry should precede evangelism and evangelism must always be the end result of ministry. Timing is important and necessary.

11. **Man of Peace:** Start with the Man of Peace or an existing relationship that will permit a Discovery Bible Study or Witness

12. **Evangelize Households/Families:** Focus on households/families, not individuals. Households include non-related people living and relating together as family.

13. **Appropriate Evangelism:** Evangelism is an intentional calling to a family to study the Word of God in order to move from not knowing God to falling in Love with Him through Jesus. The primary method used is the Discovery Bible Study in relationship with maturing believers. This makes Disciples, not Converts.+++

14. **Reproducing:** Reproducing disciples, leaders, groups and churches becomes a part of the group DNA

15. **Reaching Out (Missions):** Reaching Out to "ALL" segments of society becomes a part of the group DNA as a result of obedience to the Great Commission (missions)

16. **Redeem Local Culture (Embrace the Local Culture):** Do not import external culture, but redeem local culture by embracing all you Biblically can in a culture and transforming/redeeming the rest.

17. **Inside Leaders:** Keep all things reproducible by Inside Leaders and directed/led by Inside Leaders.

18. **Self-supporting:** Self-supporting, local leaders start and sustain all work—including groups, fellowships, and churches. Self-supporting may mean the worker has a job or does business. This improves access and breaks down the barriers between clergy and laity. It builds communities that hold each other accountable to obey the Word of God.

# 5) CHURCH PLANTING METHODS

Here are some of the proven church planting methods. They are merely a guide. The church planter needs to be exposed to these various methods but ultimately he/she needs to get the master plan from God. Note also that there is more than one method to plant a church. Locations (neighborhoods) differ, people differ (in spiritual maturity, education, etc.), and the church planter's strengths and resources differ too (evangelist, Bible teacher, counsellor, musical, etc).

In the Bible times, not one Biblical church planter was out there doing their own thing. They always related either to a mother church (such as Antioch) or the governing apostles at Jerusalem, or both.

## 1. MOTHER-CHURCH CONCEPT

Whereby one congregation breaks off part of its members and sends them to another section of town to start a new church.

## 2. A BIBLE STUDY GROUP

As people study the Word, and are nurtured in the Scriptures, they sense a growing burden to organize into a church.

## 3. BRANCH CHURCH

This method involves the mother church releasing a nucleus of people that live in the geographical vicinity of the church plant. It is designed to eventually become autonomous.

## 4. CIRCUIT CHURCH PLANTING

This model caters for situations where the population is sparse or availability of ministers is also sparse. In circuit church planting, rather than the people travelling to a central location, the minister travels from a central location. The minister may through this method cover 4 or more towns in the course of a month.

## 5. CHURCH PLANTING TEAM

There are many people within established churches that feel they want to do more for the Kingdom. Some of these people may want to formulate a church planting team that helps a church planter establish a church. Most of the team would eventually return to the mother church but from experience we have found that some became so attached to the new work that they remain. The team needs to be trained and have a very definite passion for evangelism or some other specific role in the church plant. They could specialize in music, worship leading, children's work, youth work, leading home groups, etc. It is imperative that the team works with the pastor/ church planter from the very beginning.

## 6. "CHURCH SPLIT" PLANTING (Accidental Church Planting)

Sad to say, in many places, this is the most common form of church planting. What is sad is not the new church plant, but the failure to recognize and liberate people in the body to formulate another church before disagreement sets in. Often either the new church or the old church becomes bitter over the split and they stop growing. In some cases both churches continue growing and eventually patch up their differences. This is great, but there is a lot of pain in the meantime. Churches need to recognize that God has His way of enforcing church planting on us.

## 7. ADOPTING A CHURCH

Sometimes groups of Christians or even established churches want to be adopted by a church or denomination they feel drawn to. This usually takes place because the adoptee feels that they can benefit from this new relationship. From the mother church's point of view, adoption ought to be with no strings attached. The new group needs to flow with the vision and direction that the mother church has already established.

## 8. EVANGELIST/APOSTLE CHURCH PLANTER (Catalytic church planter)

This is the model that the New Testament emphasizes the most. The evangelist or apostle has the ability to break through very quickly in a locality and build a nucleus, which becomes the foundation of a church.

## 9. PASTORAL CHURCH PLANTER (PIONEER CHURCH-PLANTING)

This is one of the most successful forms of church planting. The person who plants the church stays on to pastor it. This person usually gets a burden to plant a church in a particular area and once that is accomplished they don't feel the least bit burdened/called to repeat the endeavor elsewhere. It is as if God gives them a special ability to plant and then they get on with the job of pastoring and growing the church.

## 10. REPLANTING

Sometimes churches are kept artificially alive. There are no vital signs of life such as souls getting saved, enthusiasm, anointing, presence of God. These churches need either to be closed or replanted. Usually this is done by fresh inspirational leadership that comes in and proceeds to restructure the church.

# 6) STEPS TO CHURCH PLANTING

Most church planters do not realize how much is involved in starting a church until they have done it. Often the church begins with no name, no building, no organ, or no stationary, and in most occasions, no prospects.

Is there a formula for starting a church? No! Just as there is no perfect man to start a church. Some men look for the perfect plan thinking they cannot fail if they have the successful blueprint. But there are some general principles that church planters have used with success. The following suggestions are just that, suggestions. A church planter may use all or none of them. They are not offered as a perfect sequence, but there is some logic to their order. They are offered to help the pioneer who has a lot of zeal but no sound strategy to get started. They may need to be adapted in different areas, but they represent ideas used by other successful church planters.

1. The church planter must see the church in his mind.
2. Be sure of your call from God.
3. If married, be sure your spouse is convinced.
4. Be ready to preach and teach the Bible.
5. Know your Ecclesiology.
   No doctrine is more crucial to church planting than the doctrine of the church. The church is an assembly of baptized believers in whom Christ dwells, under the discipline of the Word of God, organized for evangelism, education, worship and fellowship, and the administering of the ordinances, and is reflected in spiritual gifts.
6. Have a Biblical Philosophy (viewpoint) of Ministry.
7. Find the right city, town, location, village, etc.
8. Determine to go first class, be unique.
   When churches begin, there is rarely enough money to do everything perfect, but the pastor should determine to do everything as best as can be done. The location, advertising, music, preaching, etc., ought to be the best that can be offered. The pastor should dress correctly. The facilities should be bright and clean. In everything the church planter must strive for quality.

9. Have a positive attitude.

10. Start a pastor-led church.

> The secret that will make your church successful and different from other fundamental churches in your area is leadership. "Everything rises or falls on leadership." Committee run churches (those controlled by the elders/deacons) rarely experience the growth of pastor-led churches. As a matter of fact, a committee, or a board of elders/deacons has rarely planted a church.

11. Enhance your walk with God (private devotions).

12. Be a soul winner.

13. Have Biblical standards for workers.

14. Learn from great men.

> Greatness in the ministry is developed by associating and learning from other great men.

15. Learn the biblical use of money.

16. Don't ask again and again the people for extra money.

> Believe in a New Testament principle of tithing and get everyone to tithe. As a result, do not get into the habit of taking many extra offerings.

17. Keep finances open.

> Make a quarterly financial report to the congregation in which all expenses are listed and explained to the congregation. However, staff salaries are not listed individually. When people have a question about the finances, it is honestly approached and answered.

18. Have a stewardship campaign the first year.

19. Give a strong Opportunity to members to pay tithe.

> Expect a congregation to tithe from the first Sunday and a new Christian to tithe when he is first saved. Many young church planters are reluctant to press their people to tithe, thinking it will run off potential members. Tithing is Christian (Malachi 3:10), therefore, expect all Christians to tithe. Unless a church is started with its members being aware of their financial obligation to God, the church will always have money problems.

20. Keep excellent financial records.

21. Survey the surrounding area/villages.

22. Choose a biblical name for the church.
23. Build a sign post for the church.
24. Find a place to live and a place to fellowship.
25. Open a church bank account if a bank is nearby.
26. Secure money support for the pastor for at least six months.
27. Gather prospective members in the area.
28. Get hymnbooks and offering baskets/plates.
29. Saturate/invade the community.
30. Set ministry goals.
31. Adopt a slogan.
    People will identify a church by its reputation, and a good slogan can help shape that reputation.
32. Visit door to door and establish a visitation programme.
33. Hold "Get Acquainted" meetings.
34. Begin prayer meetings on an off night.
35. Secure tithe cards and envelopes, and visitors cards.
36. Do not publicly attack other pastors and churches.
37. Be proud of the people in a new church.
38. Talk about each success and forget about each failure.
39. Share the/your vision with the people.
    Everything worthwhile is built on dreams.
40. Plan well the church services.
    Just because there is a small crowd that is no reason to run the church meeting without good direction. Plan each church service in an organized manner.
41. Receive an offering the very first Sunday.
42. Start a Sunday school the first Sunday.
43. Follow up visitors.
44. Begin a building fund.
45. Train personal soul winners.
46. Use authorities for credibility to the new church.

47. Support missions.

   The field is the world, not just the area in which the new church is located. As soon as possible, the new church should begin supporting missions.

48. Find land for a permanent location.

   Choose a permanent location as soon as possible. It has to be (1) easily accessible, (2) centrally located to the catchment area, (3) not chosen because the ground is inexpensive or in an undesirable location, (4) at least one –or two acres, and (5) near a residential area.

49. Build as soon as possible

50. Seek for quick financial growth.

# 7) BUILDING A HEALTHY CHURCH

What is the one thing people remember the most about their first visit to your church? With me the answer is ATMOSPHERE. They remember how the church felt. If it was warm, friendly, cold, indifferent, positive, oppressive, boring, lively, etc. First impressions do count. There is a common saying that there is no second chance to first impression. The first thing needed in building a healthy church is:

## 1. A POSITIVE ATMOSPHERE (Acts 2:44-47)

One of the best ways of having a positive atmosphere in your church is to help people feel relaxed. Members should be encouraged to participate in singing and make such singing very lively. If you have musical instruments, make sure they are in good tune. This is not to say loud music. Loud music irritates most people. It's good to have joy in church meetings.

## 2. OPEN ENTRANCES AND CLOSE EXITS

I believe that this is a Kingdom principle. If the church is designed to cater for the unchurched, then God will entrust the church with many new people. People should never be reduced to mere targets or goals. They need to be treasured as unique individuals.

A new church will grow basically from (1) New Christians, (2) Visitors, (3) Contacts of members, (4) Biological growth (Members having children).

If people feel loved and cared for, they will remain. People do stay in relatively 'dead' churches simply because they feel loved and cared for. Discipleship is one of the keys to close the church outlets.

Kill the saying that your church has a smaller front door and a wider back door, meaning that there are few people joining the church but at the same time many are leaving it going to other places. This is true with some churches. If so, make sure you know where this back door is and close it permanently. Have the marriage philosophy, "till death separates us."

## 3. A MISSION MENTALITY

Church growth and missions go together. You lose one you lose all.

## 4. AN OWNERSHIP MENTALITY

Ownership goes in something you believe in, something that grips your imagination and your passion. People will lay down their lives for ownership, certainly not for a job. They love to believe in something, something worthwhile.

## 5. PROVIDE STRONG LEADERSHIP

1 Peter 5:2-3. Leadership needs to be seen more in the light of Theocracy, which is God speaking through His ordained leaders. It has to be a motivational, inspirational, and revelation leadership.

## 6. EMPHASIZE TRAINING/TEACHING

2 Tim 2:2. The future strength of a church lies in the people that are being trained. Many leaders complain that they don't have able people to train, but most people become able only after they have been trained.

# 8) INCREASING YOUR CHURCH ATTENDANCE

Here are a few suggestions that will help churches grow. Not all will apply to every church, but maybe several of these suggestions can be adapted to your situation.

1. Offer people hope. Be positive.
2. Offer people quality preaching.
3. Offer people an exciting service.
4. Offer the Holy Spirit room to move.
5. Offer people an opportunity to be prayed for.
6. Offer people personalized pastoral care.
7. Offer people a sense of ownership.
8. Offer people a great music programme.
9. Offer people the choice of an extra service time.
10. Offer children a sense of belonging in your services.
11. Offer people special outreaches.
12. Offer people a choice of small groups (home cells) they can relate to.
13. Release your resources to where your priorities are.
14. Invite your special friends to special services.
15. Offer people a sense of consistency in the preaching and programme.
16. Once in a while conduct a week long crusade in your area.

# 9) DISCIPLESHIP

## 1. Misconceptions about Discipleship

1. Discipleship takes place when people attend church programmes.
2. Discipleship just happens.
3. Discipleship is only for new Christians.
4. Discipleship is a programme: Yet, discipleship is a lifestyle.
5. Discipleship is only for certain parts of our lives.

## 2. Definition

Discipling is an intentional relationship in which we walk alongside other disciples in order to encourage, equip and challenge one another in love to grow toward maturity in Christ. This includes equipping the disciple to teach others as well.

## 3. Meaning in Comparison

Evangelism is the transfer of the message of eternal life from one person to another. It is a once-and-for-all event.

Discipleship is the transfer of spiritual maturity from one person to another. It is a lifelong process.

"And the things that you have heard of me among many witnesses, the same commit to faithful men, who shall be able to teach others also" (2 Tim. 2:2).

## 4. Biblical Understanding of Discipleship

i. From ancient times the only way to be a disciple was to be like the teacher or master.
ii. Paul's letters to Timotheus and Titus were based on this ancient system of master and apprentice (2 Tim. 2:2, Titus 2:6-7).
iii. Paul was one of the most accomplished rabbis of his day as a disciple of the famous Gamaliel.

## 5. God's Mission — Our Mission in Relation to Discipleship

### God's Mission

a. Matthew 28:18-20 clearly teaches that the heart of our mission is to make disciples. The verbs in the passage are in participle form: going, baptizing, teaching.

Evangelism, winning people to Christ, is not fulfilling the Great Commission any more than having babies is satisfying the responsibilities of parenthood

b. God's mission: A "Great Commission" in the Old Testament (Genesis 1:26-28)

   i. Be Fruitful: reproduce your life, bear children.
   ii. Multiply: compounding effect of having children, teaching them to do the same.
   iii. Replenish the Earth: multiplication process continues until the entire earth has been filled with beings to worship and praise God (Genesis 9:1).

### Our mission

   i. Evangelism (be fruitful)
   ii. Discipleship (multiply)
   iii. Missions (replenish the earth)

   ❖ Imagine wining **1** soul every six months for 5 years
   ❖ Work out your mathematics of how many converts there will be at the end of 5 years
   ❖ A church of 100 members winning 2 souls each in a year and thoroughly discipling them. How many members will be there after twelve months?

## 6. Main Objectives in Discipleship

1. A daily walk with God in prayer and the Scriptures
2. To engage in the fellowship of believers

3. To become faithful in church attendance
4. To actively participate in service or ministry in the church

## 7. Discipleship Principles

1. Make discipleship a priority
2. See your whole life expression in terms of discipleship
3. Listen to those under discipleship
4. Address the whole of life of a disciple
5. Provide plenty of support to the disciple
6. Encourage reliance on the Holy Spirit

## 8. A Strategy to Implement Discipleship

- Have a master plan for discipleship
- Some practical suggestions
  1. Weekly contact
  2. Pray specifically
  3. Build time for social time together; Home Cells
  4. Constantly consider the four approaches:

    ➢ **Teach** - *Does the disciple understand the teachings?*

    ➢ **Train** - *Do you have an example or illustration from your own life so the disciple understands not just what to do but how to do it?*

    ➢ **Task** - *Are they taking the initiative to apply what they are learning?*

    ➢ **Team** - *What can you do together with the disciple?*

## 9. Climate to Grow Disciples

❖ Intimacy and loving accountability.

❖ Happens best in small groups.

❖ Happens best in closed groups!

**1 Thessalonians 2:8**

We loved you so much that we were delighted to share with you not only the gospel of God but our lives as well, because you had become so dear to us.

**Acts 2:42, 44**

They were continually devoting themselves to the apostles' teachings and to fellowship, to the breaking of bread and to prayer ... And all those who had believed were together and had all things in common.

**1 Peter 2:2**

Like newborn babies, long for the pure milk of the word, so that by it you may grow in respect to salvation.

# PART B: DISCIPLESHIP

This teaching is open to those who demonstrate genuine evidence of having met the risen Lord Jesus in a life-changing encounter and thereby having received Christ as Saviour and embarked on the new life journey we call the Christian life. These are the persons whose emerging walk with God will be evidenced by a favourable attitude towards Christ and an equally unfavourable attitude towards sin. The following topics of the discipleship training manual are thus aimed at establishing such believers in their new faith.

Furthermore, the discipleship discussion aims at ensuring that at the end of the training received their maturity can be measured by the fact that the emerging believers attend church regularly, that they demonstrate Christ's love by identifying with and serving other believers (Heb. 10:25; John 13:34-35; 1 John 4:20-21; Gal. 5:13), that they openly identify with clear Christian values in their lifestyle, that they manifest a heart for witnessing, that they are able to present the gospel regularly with increasing effectiveness (see Matt. 5:16; Col. 4:6; 1 Peter 3:15), that they are learners who are open and teachable (Acts 17:11) and that they are visible followers of Jesus Christ who clearly demonstrate that they live by a decidedly Christian worldview.

## 1: Assurance of Salvation

One of the first things new Christians need to know to ground their new-found faith is the assurance of their salvation. This can be explained to them using the following three points:

1)  **Salvation is *Ever-lasting*.** Salvation throughout the New Testament is called *Ever-lasting Life*. (Eg. John 3:16 and 5:24). The word used in the original manuscript means *God's Life* - without beginning, without ending! The new Christian needs to be made to understand that salvation is a spiritual joining of their spirit with the spirit of Christ that the Bible refers to as "Christ in us and we in Christ" (Rom. 6:3-5, Col. 1:27 and Gal. 2:20). An example of this is tea in hot water and hot water in tea – the two are permanently fused together! The Holy Spirit is God's invisible presence with Christians forever (Matt. 28:20). Rom. 8:9, for example, declares that we are not Christians if we do not have the Holy Spirit.

2)     **The comparison of physical and spiritual birth.** John 1:12-13 and John 3:3-7 use the comparison between physical birth and spiritual birth to give Christians a firm assurance of their salvation by explaining that neither physical birth nor spiritual birth depends on the child born but on the parents. Physical birth depends on the will of a husband and a wife and spiritual birth depends on the divine unchangeable will of God. The one thing the two births have in common is that they can never be reversed or undone! Once you are born, you are born, you cannot be unborn—both physically and spiritually!

3)     **God has permanently dealt with our sins.** We did not become saved by being good and sinless. Rom. 5:8-9 reminds Christians that *while they were yet sinners Christ died for us!* If we got saved by being good, then we can only keep our salvation by continuing to be good and we risk losing our salvation if we are no longer good but this is not what salvation is! We were not saved because we were good, but instead we were saved by God's grace so that we can become good (Eph. 2:8-9). This is why 1 John 1:8-2:2 assures Christians that when we sin, if we confess our sins, God is faithful and just to forgive us and to cleanse from all unrighteousness. The verse does not say that if we sin we will lose our salvation.

## 2: Importance of the Bible

Christians can only begin to be grounded in their faith when they are made to understand and to accept the absolute and final authority of scripture, the Bible. The Bible is the unchanging and binding divine self-revelation of God and His purposes for the human race. Unless such a foundational understanding is laid one cannot reasonably expect to make any progress in a discipleship programme. Barna points to the Bible as being the foundation of any viable discipleship exercise by saying, "It is God's inspired and accurate book for those who wish to be His followers."[1]

Although written over a period of 1500 years by more than 40 authors, the Bible has one central message—God's Salvation—with one central character—Jesus Christ, and one true author—God the Holy Spirit (2 Peter 1:21 and 2 Tim. 3:16). A second basic fact that confirms the Bible to be the

---

[1]     George Barna, *Think Like Jesus,* Nashville: Thomas Nelson, 2003, p. 46.

Word of God is the fulfillment of biblical prophecy. No other religious text in the world can make this claim (eg: Psalm 22 and Isaiah 53). A third evidential fact is that the Bible, unlike any other religious book, speaks correctly about many scientific, historical and archeological discoveries long before those discoveries were made by men. A fourth fact is that those who read the Bible and believe its message (eg: John 3:16 and Rom. 10:9-10) are changed in their character from sinners to godly persons, no matter how evil their lives had been (2 Cor. 5:17). Fifth, Jesus Christ Himself testified that the Bible is the Word of God (Matt. 5:17-19). Sixth, the Bible is God's written Word and Jesus Christ, God the Son, is God's Word in flesh and blood (John 1:1-2 and 14) so that through the Bible, the written Word, God the Son, the living Word, working with God the Holy Spirit, brings us to God the Father (John 14:6). J.I. #Packer puts this truth succinctly by saying, "The written Word of the Lord leads us to the living Lord of the Word, and our attitude to Him is effectively our choice of destiny."[2] A seventh strong evidence that the Bible is the Word of God is the fact that Christians can personally testify to the truth of the Bible from their own very real experience of salvation, and they can also testify that God answers prayer just as promised in the Bible (1 John 5:14-15).

## 3: Bible Study

Having established the authority of the Bible as the non-negotiable Word of God, Christians must then be taught the importance of personal Bible Study and made to understand that the systematic and careful study of the Word of God, the Bible, is the spiritual milk they need to take in daily to grow in their new faith much as a new born baby needs its mother's breast milk (1 Peter 2:2).

This is precisely what was done at the birth of the New Testament church to ensure the spiritual growth and vitality of the early church. What Acts 2:42 calls "the Apostles' teaching" can be likened to Bible Study because what the Apostles taught these early Christians then is what we have in both the Old and the New Testaments of our Bibles today. The Apostles taught the early Christians exactly what they had learned from Jesus Christ, especially after His resurrection. In Luke 24:27 and 44 Jesus explained to the disciples

---

[2]  J.I. Packer, *Knowing God*, Downers Grove: InterVarsity Press, 1973, p. 20.

after His resurrection that the entire OT had really been about Him and the work of redemption he had just accomplished on the cross.

The basic purpose of Bible study is to discover the facts and details in a Bible text and to draw conclusions about the applicable meaning of the text. This requires observation, interpretation, and application. Observation means reading and re-reading a text until we become so acquainted with it that we can confidently answer the questions: What does this passage say? What is the actual content in the text? Who was writing? To whom was the message originally written? Who are the people involved in the scenario? What's happening? What's said? Is it a command, an exhortation, a rebuke, a question, an answer, a prayer, a quotation of other scripture, or something else? What's the main point? What key words or phrases are used? What's the context? What literary style is being used? Is it narrative, conversation, parable, prophecy, poetry, a letter, or a sermon? Are there time references? Are there words related to the past, present, or future? Are there locations mentioned—towns, roads, rivers, mountains, regions, or other landmarks? Are there any clues about why things are being said or done? Is there an explanation about how things are done?[3]

Interpretation is determining the meaning of a text. Stein notes, "Biblical interpretation involves not just understanding the specific conscious meaning of the author but also the principle or pattern of meaning he sought to communicate."[4] Interpretation answers the basic question of what God meant by what He said in the passage through the biblical author. The task of the Christian is to therefore discover the original intent and meaning of the biblical author because the interpretation of the Bible is not a matter of personal opinion, personal feelings or democratic agreement; it's a matter of gathering evidence from the text and following established principles of interpretation. In 2 Timothy 2:15 Paul speaks of the need for Christians to be precise and accurate in interpreting the Bible so that it all fits together without any contradiction.

---

[3]   Robert M. West, *How to Study the Bible*, Ulrichsville, OH: Barbour Publishing, 2007, p. 40.

[4]   Robert H. Stein, *A Basic Guide to Interpreting the Bible*, Grand Rapids, MI: Baker Academic, 1994, p. 27.

Having explained the meaning and importance of observation and inter-pretation in Bible study the next topic naturally has to address the understanding and the application of the Bible to the life of the Christian. Paul explains in 2 Timothy 3:16-17 that in the life of a Christian the inspired Word of God is profitable for doctrine, for reproof, for correction, for instruction in righteousness. In other words the Bible is invaluable divine knowledge to believe, to use as God's perfect standard of right and wrong, for being restored after we have sinned and for remaining restored in our relationship with God. These four spiritual benefits are to make believers complete so that they can do whatever God has called them to do.

The goal of Bible study isn't only gaining biblical information, but also experiencing the transformation of our worldviews. Christians do not only seek to get through the Bible, but rather that the Bible gets through to them. This means that, as we study the Bible, we apply it to our lives by being determined that if there's a good example, we will follow it, if there's a warning, we will heed it, if there's a command, we will obey it, and if there's a promise, we will believe it.[5] This is what James 1:22 means when it calls for Christians to be doers of the Word and not only hearers.

## 4: The Lordship of Christ

Becoming a Christian means that we have accepted by faith deep within our hearts that Jesus has given His life for us on the cross in death so that we can give him our life so that He becomes our new owner. Paul explains this by saying in 1 Cor. 6:19-20, "Do you not know that your body is a temple of the Holy Spirit, who is in you, whom you have received from God? You are not your own, you were bought at a price." When we got born again we became the property of the Lord and He became our Master. By right of redemption Christians are God's property and we completely belong to Him.

The sober implication of this is that because on the day we became Christians, we became God's property and we can no longer consider ourselves to be our own masters. Instead we must learn to acknowledge in

---

[5]    Howard G. and William D. Hendricks, *Living by the Book: Principles for Christian Living from the Bible to Live By*, Chicago: Moody Press, 1991, p. 304-306.

everything God's ownership and authority, and we can only legitimately function in every area of our lives with reference to our new owner, Christ. In Gal. 2:20 Paul's statement that "I am crucified with Christ" means that the old sinful person we were before we came to Christ is dead and a new person, now under new management, has come into being. Paul explains this in 2 Cor. 5:17 to mean that Christians are "a new creation, the old has passed away, the new has come!"

Jesus taught His disciples this important truth of the Christian life in Luke 9:23-24 when he said, "If anyone would come after me, he must take up his cross daily and follow me. For whosoever wants to save his life will lose it, but whoever loses his life for me will save it. What good is it for a man to gain the whole world and lose his own soul?" By the expression "take up his cross" Christ meant that on every single day of a Christian's life we must remember that on the day we got born again our old self died with Christ on the cross (Gal. 2:20) and our life is now new (2 Cor. 5:17) so that we now belong completely to Christ. Jesus Christ is not only our *Saviour* but also our *Lord*, who, in the words of Berkhof, "rules and protects His church and governs the universe."[6]

## 5: The Will of God

An important part of the process of growing into Christian maturity is getting to know and to do the will of God. This awareness of knowing and doing God's will needs to be reflected in all the important decisions in the life of a maturing Christian. In John 10:27 Jesus said, "My sheep hear my voice." This means that the Christian has been provided with inner spiritual ears with which to "hear" the voice of God and to discern His divine will in most important matters. The New Testament teaches that Christ lives in the Christian by the Holy Spirit (Eph. 1:13 and 2 Cor. 1:21-22). This means that God has placed His voice within us and has given to the Christian the ability and the facility to hear from Him. Again, Rom. 8:14 and John 16:13 indicate that the Christian is led by the Holy Spirit and this can only be true if we can "hear" the one leading us!

---

[6]   Louis Berkhof, *A Summary of Christian Doctrine*. Edinburgh: Banner of Truth Trust, 2005, p. 78.

The Bible presents us with several ways in which God enables us to hear Him to impart to us His will for our daily Christian lives. One way is that a Christian can experience a strong impression in the mind that is almost audible of a statement from scripture pointing or offering an indication of a particular course of action. This can happen unexpectedly at any time of the Lord's choosing, be it during a personal devotion, in a church service or even in a dream as the Christian is asleep (Num. 12:6 and Job 33:15-18). This is often confirmed as being a communication from the Lord by an accompanying sense of internal calm and peace. If there is no sense of inner peace, then it is likely that this is not from the Lord but from the Christian's own mind. Another way is that Christians can be led to discern the will of God is through circumstances. This requires caution because Satan or the Christian's own carnal desires can draw them away from the true will of God. Christians must, in such cases, ensure that the internal witness of the Holy Spirit, the sense of inner peace, and above all, conformity with the Word of God, are all in place. As Derek Prince notes, "The Word of God is the supreme standard by which all else must be judged and tested. No revelation is to be accepted if it is not in full accord with the word of God."[7]

## 6: The Need for Prayer

Barna notes that, "Jesus spent time alone with God seeking solitude to hear the voice of His Father in Heaven … to remind Himself to focus on God … He prayed constantly for guidance."[8] In the gospel accounts that give us a record of His earthly life, particularly in the Gospel of Luke, Jesus is indeed presented as a man of prayer. Luke 5:16 Luke tells us that Jesus often withdrew to quiet places to pray. In Luke 6:12 and 13 we see Jesus in an entire night of prayer seeking guidance from the Father. In Luke 9:28 we see Jesus retreating with Peter, James and John to a mountain to pray. In John 17, on the night He was betrayed, we read of Jesus' long and holy priestly prayer for all of us.

By his repeated focus on Jesus as a man of prayer, Luke draws us to the

---

[7] Derek Prince, *Faith to Live By*, Fort Lauderdale, FL: Derek Prince Ministries, 1977, p. 37.

[8] George Barna, *Think Like Jesus,* Nashville: Thomas Nelson, 2003, p. 7.

unavoidable conclusion that if he, the infallible Son of God, needed to pray so much, how much more so for Christians today, who are weak and fallible creatures, often led astray by the self-life and so easily prone to sin and weariness! Prime states, "Prayer is the principal expression of our relationship to God through Jesus Christ" (Prime, 58).

Through His prayer life Jesus demonstrated to Christians that prayer has been designed by God to be one of the primary ways in which He interacts with us to develop a relationship of intimacy with us. As with developing a close relationship with another person, if we are to get to know God on a personal intimate level and grow in our faith, we need to spend time with Him by cultivating inflexible personal habits of prayer, daily talking to Him and listening to Him (James 4:8).

## 7: The Quiet Time

This topic aims to teach Christians to personalize prayer in their lives by observing a quiet time of personal prayer each day, emphasizing, as noted above, that Jesus must be our example in all things, especially as relates to His prayer life.

Christians need to be reminded that Jesus practiced a quiet time by waking up very early in the morning each day to pray. Mark 1:35 reveals to us that Jesus woke up well before the break of day to pray. Although the Bible does not command us explicitly to wake up and pray in the morning hours, because we are often tired at night from the day's work and struggles and because at night one is likely to have one's thoughts crowded with the events of the day, it is wiser to set aside the very early morning hours for one's quiet time, because at that time, after a restful night's sleep, one is fresh and alert.

The importance and the many spiritual benefits of the quiet time cannot be emphasized enough. By observing the quiet time we present to God the sacrifice of the first-fruits of each day, when the day is still new, fresh and undisturbed. When we observe a quiet time of prayer, God blesses us with a special dispensation of grace and renewed inner strength to face the challenges of each new day, like the manna the children of Israel collected in the early morning of each day in the wilderness (Exodus 16:14-16 and 21).

Besides Jesus Christ himself many other biblical characters also observed the quiet time. These include Abraham, Jacob, Moses, Joshua, Gideon, Hannah, Samuel, David, Job and the Apostles as shown in such passages as Gen. 19:27, 21:14, 22:3, 28:18, Ex. 8:20, 9:13, 24:4, 34:4, Joshua 3:1, 6:12, 7:16, 8:18, Judges 6:38, 1 Sam 1:19, 15:12, 17:20, Job 1:5, Psalms 5:3, 108:2-3, 63:1, 119:147-148, 143:8 and 78:34. Again, throughout the history of the church, we discover that all the Christian men and women whom God has used mightily had a habit of waking up early to commune with the Lord in prayer, Bible study and worship. These include Christian leaders such as John (Praying) Hyde, Hudson Taylor, John Wesley, Charles Spurgeon, A.W. Tozer, David Brainard and Watchman Nee.

The benefits of cultivating a quiet time of prayer for the Christians are indeed incalculable. The well-known American church leader and pastor, John Ortberg, upon adopting this lifestyle of prayer, writes, "I was amazed by the uniqueness of praying at night. There was a stillness that was never available during the day. In the darkness and the eerie silence I felt as if I was actually 'keeping watch' with Jesus. And in keeping watch with Him, I found rest for my soul."[9]

## 8: Personal Testimony

Any effective discipleship programme will doubtless encourage Christians to share their personal testimony of salvation with friends and family. This will help them to reflect deeply about what God has done in their life and also enable them to share their salvation story simply and clearly with others.

Eims counsels that in sharing their personal testimony, Christians should observe the following common sense rules: First, to make it personal, not to preach. Second, simply tell what Christ has done for them, using the pronouns "I", "me", "my", and "mine". Third, to make it short, noting that three or four minutes should be enough time to deal with the essential facts. Fourth, to keep Christ central in one's narrative, always highlighting what Christ has done for you personally. Fifth, to always use the Word of God since a verse or two of Scripture will add power to your story, and,

---

[9]   John Ortberg, "The Last Taboo," *Leadership Journal*, Vol. XV No. 2, 1994, p. 82.

finally, to make the story of your conversion so clear that another person hearing it would know how to receive Christ.

In sharing their testimony Christians should do so sequentially and systematically by saying first something about their life before they trusted Jesus Christ; then recounting their conversion and how they came to trust Him, and then something of what it has meant to know Christ such as the blessings of sins forgiven, the assurance of eternal life, and other important ways in which their life and worldview have changed.

As they are encouraged to share their personal testimony Christians need to be reminded that they do not have the power in themselves nor their words to convince anyone of spiritual truth and that it is the Holy Spirit who convicts non-Christians of their need to know Christ (John 16:8). It is also necessary to explain to them that in sharing their personal testimony they need to ask God to honour the proclamation of His Word, to convince people of their need, and to strengthen them as they share their story and the gospel with others.[10]

## 9: Christian Fellowship

The cardinal importance of Christian fellowship in the life of Christians was demonstrated by the experience of the new Christians at the birth of the New Testament church in Acts 2 where verses 44 and 45 say, "All the believers had everything in common. Selling their possessions and goods, they gave to anyone as he had need." The tangible experiential demonstration of Christian fellowship described in this passage translated into real life what Jesus Christ had taught the Apostles about loving one another. The Apostles understood that they were the *Body of Christ* and that this meant that true Christian fellowship could be compared to the human body whereby every member needs the other members to function as they should.

The essence of Christian fellowship is sharing with one another of our joys, our hopes, our concerns, our fears and our difficulties. We do this to

---

[10] Leroy Eims, "The Lost Art of Disciple Making" in *Readings and Resource Materials for Developing a Christian Worldview*, Springfield, MI: Global University, 2005, p. 88.

encourage one another, to counsel one another, to stand with one another, even to correct one another and also to be very real and human and vulnerable with one another in the context of the church community. Very often church relationships are not as nourishing and building as they should be with no real reaching out to one another. Sadly this means that Christians often suffer and agonize in isolation in their difficulties when there very well may be other Christians who would gladly assist them and pray with them and encourage them if they knew what they were going through. This was not the case in the early church. The very existence of the church as a company of people who had a personal relationship with God through Jesus Christ was a new experience for them all and they needed each other for mutual encouragement and support.

Christians need to understand that, because their Christian worldview will often put them at odds with the values and worldview of their non-Christian friends and relatives, it is vitally important for them to meet regularly with like-minded brothers and sisters in Christ to encourage, to edify and to strengthen one another as was done in the early church (Eph. 5:19, Col. 3:16, Heb. 10:24-25 and 1 Cor. 14:26).

## 10: Sin and Victory over it

The new birth does not mean that sin as a principle is rooted out and removed or eradicated from the life of a Christian. Sin is still very present in the heart of the Christian and if given the opportunity sin will overpower us and cause us to sin again, whether consciously or unconsciously. Indeed, the mark of a true Christian is not sinless perfection but instead a very strong inner sense of deep remorse over sin. 1 John 3:9 and 5:18 explain that a person who claims to be a Christian but continues to sin willfully and happily without any appreciable sense of remorse is not truly born again.

Christians need to be warned about the serious consequences of sin. Isaiah 59:2, for example, tells us that sin disrupts our fellowship with God and Eph. 4:26 explains that sin gives the devil a foothold in the lives of Christians and allows him to deceive us and to bring needless difficulties and frustrations into our lives. Again, Gal. 6:7-8 teaches us that sin can bring real physical, material suffering into our lives and Galatians 5:19-21 also warns us that when Christians entertain sin in their lives they deprive themselves of the spiritual and even the material blessings and benefits of our salvation, referred to in this passage as "the kingdom of God". In his epistles Paul frequently refers to Christians who entertain sin in their lives as "not inheriting the kingdom of God." In Gal. 5:19-21, after listing some of the sins Christians can fall prey to such as sexual immorality, drunkenness, selfish ambition, fits of rage, jealousy, envy and greed, Paul then goes on to list in Galatians 5:22-24 some of the blessings of salvation which are love, joy, peace, goodness, kindness, faith, gentleness, patience and self-control. Paul calls these blessings the fruit of the Spirit. They describe the character of Christ, who lives in us by His Holy Spirit, so that these character traits progressively become ours as we learn to walk with God in faith and obedience. Brown says, "The fruit of the Spirit encompasses the believer's relationship with God, with his fellow human beings, and with himself."[11]

Of great importance to Christians is the knowledge of how to experience victory over sin in their lives. In Romans 8:1-2 Paul describes the anatomy of Christian victory over sin as the "Law of the Spirit of Life in Christ Jesus" that overcomes the "Law of Sin and Death." The word *law* is commonly defined as any unavoidable and non-negotiable system of rules that regulate human actions and behaviour. This can apply to natural, physical laws such as the law of gravity and also to judicial laws that are the rules and regulations that govern human behaviour and are enforced by governing authorities to ensure that there is justice and order in society. In Romans 8:1-2 Paul describes the two laws at work in the life of the Christian as the "Law of the Spirit of life in Christ Jesus" and "the Law of Sin and Death" and declares that the higher and stronger of these two laws, the Law of the Spirit of life in Christ Jesus, overcomes on behalf of the Christian who draws on this by faith, the Law of sin and death.

Paul's prescription for overcoming sin works when Christians are confronted with a temptation to sin and they choose to adopt a faith attitude based on their trust in the fact that the life and strength of Christ is in them (Gal. 2:20) to impart to them whatever particular strength they need to overcome that sin or temptation. As they regularly learn to make

---

[11] George W. Brown, *The Fruit of the Spirit,* Grantham: Stanborough Press, 1998, p. 11.

this faith choice in every situation of temptation, Christians can draw on the inner strength of Christ within them to overcome temptation and sin (Phil. 4:13). Paul evidently found this to be the solution to overcoming sin in his own life because Romans 8:1-2 follows Romans 7:15-24 where he describes the awful dilemma of the Christian struggle against sin and he offers Romans 8:1-2 as the solution to the intractable sin problem.

Concurring with this, Ferguson further explains that Paul's prescription is based on the fact that the Christian's victory over sin is accomplished through union with Christ which leads to a new life of spiritual vitality because our union with Christ involves the death of "the sinful old man."[12]

## 11: Faith

Faith plays a defining role in the Christian life. First, there is the basic faith the Christian needs to receive salvation that is imparted to us as a gift of God (Eph. 2:8, John 6:44-45, John 16:8-90), when the Holy Spirit convicts us of sin, imparts faith into us and brings us to accept Christ and to be reconciled to God. Notes Derek Prince, "Faith is the first and indispensable response of the human soul in its approach to God."[13] Second, there is the faith Christians require to walk with God in daily victory and to enter into the fullness of the blessings God has in store for His children. About this, Prince observes that, "As we maintain our relationship with God through faith, we are enabled to endure and to overcome the tests and hardships that confront us in our daily Christian lives."[14]

The English Dictionary defines the word *faith* as "complete trust or confidence in someone or something." The biblical definition of faith found in Heb. 11:1 confirms that biblical faith is an attitude of trust in someone or something which allows that thing or person to act on our behalf. This means that faith is as an attitude towards an object or person and the most

---

[12] Sinclair B. Ferguson, *The Christian Life*, Edinburgh: Banner of Truth Trust, 1989, p. 134-142.

[13] Derek Prince, *Faith to Live By*, Fort Lauderdale, FL: Derek Prince Ministries, 1977, p. 54.

[14] Derek Prince, *Faith to Live By*. Fort Lauderdale, FL: Derek Prince Ministries, 1977, p. 15.

important thing about faith, then, is not the *quantity* of faith we have but the *reliability* of the object or person in which we place our faith. This is what Jesus was seeking to explain in Matt. 17:20 when He referred to faith as small as seed of mustard seed—although small in size, it is effective because it is placed in an all-powerful God. When Jesus reprimanded His disciples by saying *O ye of little faith*, He was referring to the *inconsistency* of their faith, not its *size*.

Derek Prince concurs with this understanding of faith by noting that "Faith is the one thing that relates us to the unseen realities of God and His Word. Faith lifts us above the realm of our own ability and makes God's possibilities available to us."[15]

## 12: Love

In John 13:34-35 Jesus said to His disciples, "A new commandment I give you. Love each other as much as I love you." This command echoes throughout the New Testament. In 1 Corinthians 13:13 Paul referred to love as the greatest and most desirable of all the Christian virtues. In the Christian life, then, love is not an option—it is a necessary requirement. The common English Dictionary definition of the word *love* is, "An intense feeling of deep affection for someone or something or a deep romantic or sexual attachment to someone." In the New Testament, however, when Christians are called upon to love, unlike this common understanding of the word, it is not a call for us to engage our *feelings* but instead to engage our *will* through our actions, with or without feelings. This is because in many New Testament passages the word *love* is a translation of the Greek word *Agape*. This stands in sharp contrast to the meaning of two other Greek words that are also translated in the NT as *love*, which are *Eros and Phileo*.

*Eros* is most commonly used to describe the affection that spouses have for each other and is conditional upon the one loved because it is based on the desirability of the object of my love that *draws out* my love. *Phileo* refers to brotherly or friendship affection that relates to our siblings or school or work mates. As with *Eros*, *Phileo* is also conditional because it depends on

---

[15] Derek Prince, *Faith to Live By*. Fort Lauderdale, FL: Derek Prince Ministries, 1977, p. 15.

our sharing a commonality of bonding experiences with the persons we *phileo,* such as having the same parents, sharing the same home, attending the same school, sharing the same workplace or sharing the same interests.

*Agape* is the word that is used when Christians are called to love one another in the New Testament; however, it is very different from *eros* and *phileo* because *Agape* refers to God's completely unconditional love for us. In 1 John 4:8 and 16 the Apostle John declares that *God is love*—God doesn't just *have* love, He *is* love! J.I. Packer, in his classic book, *Knowing God*, says this about these two verses from 1 John, "St. John's twice-repeated statement, "God is love" is one of the most tremendous utterances in the whole Bible."[16] *Agape* refers to God loving us not because of who we are or what we are, but rather because of who He is and what He is. This is why *Agape* is defined not by *feelings* but by *actions* and God's own supreme example of this is described in John 3:16: as, "For God so loved the world that He gave His only begotten Son." God's action of *giving* His only begotten Son expressed His *Agape* for us.

The key to the Christian's ability to obey the New Testament command to love, to *agape,* is provided by Paul in Romans 5:5 where he states that when we become Christians "the love of God is poured out in our hearts through the Holy Spirit who is given to us." In Gal. 5:22, again, Paul notes that *the fruit of the Spirit* (the character traits that the Holy Spirit imparts into our lives) are love, joy, peace, kindness, patience, goodness, faith, gentleness and self-control. These are the character traits of Christ Himself imparted to us by His Holy Spirit, and it is this life of Christ in us that empowers us to live and to love the way Christ lived and loved, and I believe that it was for this reason that in John 13:34-35 Christ expected His disciples to love one another as He had loved them.

## 13: Giving

The supreme example of giving in the Bible is provided by God himself in John 3:16, where it says that He *gave* to sinful humans His only begotten Son Jesus Christ to die for us to take away our sins and reconcile us to God. As with the call to love, therefore, in the New Testament, Christians are

---

[16] J.I. Packer, *Knowing God*, Downers Grove, IL: InterVarsity Press, 1973, p. 106.

called to emulate God's example of giving by being characterized by their giving. Tithing and offerings (Malachi 3:1-10) are part of what God commands believers to always take part in with the understanding that "it is more blessed to give than to receive."

Many reasons are provided for this call. The first of these is that God the Holy Spirit comes to live inside the Christian at re-birth and it is to be expected that Christians will begin to reflect God's character trait of giving in our own lives. This is why giving is such an instinctive Christian reality and everywhere when Christians take the profession of their faith seriously they almost instinctively give to those in need around them, as was done in the early church (Acts 4:32-35). O'Donovan states, "In the historical growth of the Christian church throughout the world, the majority of the first converts to Christ in every community have come from people who were helped by other Christians in ways they could understand."[17]

A second reason is that giving is a practical, tangible demonstration of Christians' recognition that everything they own belongs to God and that God has committed Himself to provide for them. An example of this is the story of the widow's mite in Luke 21:4 and Mark 12:41-44. The widow's practical demonstration of faith in God's commitment to meet her needs found Christ's high commendation. A third reason is that Christians are called to give as an expression of their understanding that, although we do not merit or deserve anything from God, He has freely and abundantly given to us everything we need for life and salvation and for this reason we too should give to others what we have so freely received from God. It seems clear that God is looking for faithful men and women who will be open channels for His giving to a needy world, and if we choose to be those open channels, we ourselves will naturally never lack (Luke 6:38)!

## 14: Obedience

Throughout the Bible obedience to God and to God's revealed will is shown to be a cardinal requirement for growth in our relationship with God, and Christians are called to demonstrate complete and unswerving obedience

---

[17] Wilbur O'Donovan, *Biblical Christianity in African Perspective.* Carlisle, UK: Paternoster Press, 1996, p. 63.

to the Lord's guidance and direction, even when it doesn't make human sense to do so (1 Sam 15:22 and 2 John 6).

In the Old Testament a good demonstration of this is the life of Joshua. In Joshua 5:13-15 we find Joshua seeking to employ human strategies and military intelligence to devise ways in which the children of Israel could attack Jericho, the first city of importance they encountered in Canaan, which was surrounded by tightly-shut and seemingly impregnable high walls. Joshua is then confronted by the Lord in the form of the Captain of the Host of the Lord, whom Bible scholars believe was a pre-incarnate theophany of the Lord Jesus Christ. The Lord appeared to Joshua because only God could provide the most viable method for the fulfillment of His divine promise to give the Israelites victory over the Canaanites. Joshua, in keeping with his tendency to obey, quickly fell in line to obey the Lord even when the Lord's instructions on how they were to overcome Jericho did not make sense. Joshua's obedience enabled the children of Israel to gain complete victory over the inhabitants of Canaan (Joshua 10:42 and Joshua 11:23).

As with the Old Testament Joshua, so it was with our ultimate Testament Joshua himself, Jesus Christ, who "learned obedience from what He suffered" (Heb. 5:8), setting an example once for all for all Christians who seek to make progress in their walk with God. Obedience is a key indicator of a Christian's growth and maturity and a sure measure of the successful fulfillment of God's purposes for our lives.

## 15: The Use of Time

Christians who seek to grow and mature in their faith will do well to heed Paul's counsel to the Christians in Eph. 5:16 (KJV) *to redeem the time*, because the days are evil. Here are seven suggestions for how this can be done:

1) *To be faithful stewards of God's time.* In 1 Cor. 4:2 the scriptures admonish us to be faithful stewards of all of God's resources entrusted to us. Time is among the most valuable of God's resources entrusted to us.

2) *Establishing clearly defined goals.* Christians who are aware of God's specific expectations for their lives do well to establish clearly defined goals which will direct their daily work and efforts and their use of time.

3) *Planning time schedules.* Making time schedules to meet one's work obligations and priorities will help Christians to use their time well. These time schedules can comprise of daily, weekly and monthly time planning sheets.

4) *Forming fruitful habits of doing routine things.* This enables daily unavoidable routines to have their place in one's time-keeping without detracting from the more important major tasks of the day.

5) *Setting deadlines.* This will enable Christians to attend to important assignments and to do so in a timely and effective manner.

6) *Learning to say "No".* There are times when Christians need to remember that their time is to be used for what God has *called them to do* and not merely for what *they can do*. This often requires them to be able to say "no" to seemingly good activities which, carefully reviewed, will be seen to rob them of time for more fruitful ministry.

7) *Setting aside time for family.* A common failure of many Christians is not making enough time for their families. This can cause them to be distracted and ineffective and to lose the power of their witness when their families become dysfunctional.

## 16: Witnessing

In Acts 1:8, in one of the risen Christ's final interactions with His disciples before His ascension, He said to them, "But you will receive power when the Holy Spirit comes on you; and you will be my witnesses in Jerusalem, and in all Judea and Samaria, and to the ends of the earth." The Greek word that has been translated in this verse as witness is *martureo* that means *to be a witness* or *to bear witness*. The English word *witness* is commonly defined as a person who sees or experiences an incident or event on a first-hand basis. In Acts 1:8, therefore, Jesus Christ was commissioning His disciples to go and bear witness to the world about what they had personally seen and experienced of His life, death and resurrection. This command has come to be known as the Great Commission. It is a non-negotiable call to all Christians everywhere at all times to be involved in bearing witness to the life-changing and life-transforming power of the good news of salvation through Jesus Christ.

Christians bear witness to the gospel by word and by deed. In Matthew 5:13 and 14 Jesus called His disciples "the salt of the earth" and "the light of the world." Salt is a *preservative* and a *seasoning* agent. Jesus used salt to symbolize the role of Christians in society as those who *preserve* God's will in a world characterized by godlessness. Our Christian lives *season* the world for God by re-presenting His truth and righteousness to the world (Col. 4:5-6 and 1 Peter 1:12). Salt preserves and seasons *silently* but *effectively.* The gospel, like salt, works effectively by demonstrating the practicality of the message we proclaim. This happens when we proclaim the gospel *silently* by the example of our *godly lives* rather than by *word*, because our godly Christian lives make a powerful impression on non-believers. Such examples are often a means of preparing their hearts for the gospel message itself. Our lives proclaim the gospel we preach. God has summoned each Christian to be a witness of what he has "seen and heard" (1 John 1:3). Witnessing is a style of living and we do well to remember that Christians are a witness at all times by their lives because actions speak louder than words.

Jesus Christ, Himself "the light of the world" (John 8:12), referred to His disciples as "the light of the world" because they bear the light of Christ that dispels the darkness of sin and ignorance about God. In the NT Christians are likened to being in the light and non-Christians are said to be darkness or to be in darkness—the darkness of Sin, Self and Satanic control (John 3:19 and Eph. 5:8). The Gospel brings the light of God into the lives of human beings to bring them out of the darkness of sin into the light of God (1 Peter 2:9). As Christians we minister as children of light by preaching the Gospel of Christ both corporately and individually.

The disciples received the Holy Spirit primarily to empower them to fulfill Jesus' great command—to proclaim the gospel to all nations (John 20:21-23 and Acts 1:8), and the spiritual dynamic for witnessing for Christ today remains the Holy Spirit's enablement (Matthew 28:20, Luke 24:48, Acts 1:8). Packer notes that William Temple, former Archbishop of Canterbury, defines Christian witnessing and evangelism as: "Presenting Jesus Christ in the power of the Holy Spirit so that men might come to trust Him as Saviour and serve Him as Lord in the fellowship of His Church."[18]

It is worth noting that the verbal act of witnessing involves showing non-Christians the way back to God, and we do this by telling them to: (1) *Believe in Jesus* (John 3:16 & Acts 16:31) and we explain to them that believing in Jesus means that we accept who He says He is, and we accept by faith His redemptive work on the cross on our behalf. (2) *Repent of sin* (Acts 2:38 & Acts 3:19). (3) *Ask for and receive forgiveness* (1 John 1:9). (4) *Accept and Acknowledge* (John 1:12 and Rom. 10:9-10) and (5) *Follow Jesus* (Luke 9:23) through obedient discipleship that involves cultivating regular habits of prayer and Bible study.

## 17: Satan

Ephesians 6:11-12 speaks of the Christian's struggle against "the devil's schemes" and against "the rulers" and "the powers of this dark world and against the spiritual forces of evil in the heavenly realms." Although throughout the Bible we are given such hints, nowhere does the Bible give us a clear explanation of Satan's origins. More importantly, though, Satan is presented in the Bible as a creature of God, not an alternative God, because the Bible explains clearly enough that there is only one true eternal God, not two Gods in the universe, battling it out.

Some Bible scholars speculate from Ezek. 28:11-19 and Isaiah 1412-14 that Satan was created by God as an arch-angel in heaven called Lucifer who was in control of other angels, probably one third of the angels. Exalted by God, when he tried to go higher than God had decreed for him, God expelled him from heaven together with the hosts of angels who were under his control and who rebelled with him.[19] In Luke 10:18 Jesus was probably referring to this defeat of Satan in heaven in the dim and undefined biblical past. We also have a hint in 1 Tim. 3:6 where Paul notes that pride and conceit led to Satan's downfall and judgment. In Rev. 12:9 and in John 8:44 Satan is also called "the great dragon" or "the serpent of

---

[18]   J.I. Packer, *Knowing God*, Downers Grove: InterVarsity Press, 1973, p. 37.

[19]   Judy Wadge, *Be a Winner: Principles of Spiritual Warfare*, Nairobi: Life Challenge Africa, 2006, p. 19.

old who deceives the whole world," "a murderer from the beginning," "a liar and the father of lies." These names and descriptions seem to reflect Satan's deception of our first parents in the Garden of Eden (Gen. 3).

The Bible's portrayal of Satan as this fallen angel is that he is definitely not omnipresent, omnipotent, or omniscient but relies instead on a host of evil, unrepentant forces (Eph. 6:11-12) who form his kingdom and are evidently divided into various hierarchies. It appears that Satan also has under his control hosts of demons, also called evil spirits, who are not angels because they do not have bodies but instead often seek to enter and dwell in the human body, or in animals as we see in the story of the Gaderene demoniac in Mark 5:1-17.

Eph. 4:26 makes it clear that sin gives Satan a foothold in the lives of Christians that allows him to deceive us and to bring needless difficulties and frustrations into our lives. Judy Wadge says, "It is very important to know the truth about what the Bible says concerning Satan and his demons ... because if we fail to understand the satanic source of some of our problems, we will not know how to deal with them."[20]

## 18: Christian Leadership

Christian leadership entails the concept of the leader as a servant who leads and a leader who serves,[21] the leader as a shepherd who guides and protects the people of God and the leader as a steward who cares for the sheep that Christ, the Chief and Good Shepherd (John 10:14 & I Peter 5:4), has entrusted to him.[22] Jesus Christ Himself is our supreme example who embodied these biblical characteristics of a servant leader (#??22:27 and Matt. 20:28).

In the African context, sadly, traditional concepts of leadership embrace the ideas of might, material wealth and worldly wisdom as being the requisite

---

[20] Judy Wadge, *Be a Winner: Principles of Spiritual Warfare*, Nairobi: Life Challenge Africa, 2006, p. 18.

[21] Harris W. Lee, *Effective Church Leadership: A Practical Sourcebook*, Silver Springs, MD: Ministerial Association, GCSDA, 2003, p. 97.

[22] Edgar J. Elliston, *Home Grown Leaders*, Pasadena: William Carey Library, 1992, p. 23-24.

qualifications and expressions of admirable leadership.[23] Influenced by these notions of leadership, Christian leadership in the African context displays values and attitudes that are often intolerant, nepotistic, autocratic and inconsiderate of the real and felt needs of the people they lead. Elliston describes this as "the misuse of influence" and the unfortunate effects of this misuse of influence and ungodly leadership, as Elliston observes, are "church decline, splits, spiritual barrenness, ineffectiveness, jealousy, envy, factions and strife".[24]

What is needed to bring about true Christian leadership in the African context is the adoption of what Elliston describes as "leadership models for the church drawn from the scriptures and evaluated in terms of accountability to Christ".[25] Christian leadership, in other words, is best exemplified by following a biblical model that imitates Christ's own servant leadership and it is only the adoption of these biblical principles of Christian leadership that can ensure that the African church will be both effective and Christ-like and able to accomplish God's intended purposes for His church on this continent.

**Conclusion**

The early church conquered the Roman Empire not through fighting with weapons of war nor because the early Christians successfully advocated for and received their due human rights, the freedom of worship nor the freedom of unhindered public expression of their faith. The biblical record is that in the face of severe persecutions the early Christians stood firm and uncompromising in their faith because they knew and clearly understood who and what they believed through the systematic teaching of sound biblical doctrine (2 Tim. 1:12 and 2 Tim. 3:16) and that this knowledge was carefully and systematically passed on to them through the effective discipleship programme of their leaders (Acts 2:42-47). Observes Deek

---

[23] Tokunbo Adeyemo, "Leadership" in *Africa Bible Commentary*, Nairobi: WordAlive, 2006, p. 546.

[24] Edgar J. Elliston, *Home Grown Leaders*, Pasadena: William Carey Library, 1992, p. 18.

[25] Edgar J. Elliston, *Home Grown Leaders*, Pasadena: William Carey Library, 1992, p. 22.

Prince, "The early Christians not only believed, but they also *knew*. They had an experiential faith that produced a definite knowledge of that which they believed."[26]

It is my conviction that, if the church will adopt the same approach to the urgent need to disciple Christians in the church today, that will use a discipleship training manual such as is discussed in this book, a solidly Christian worldview and the same unwavering witness to Christ that the early church so admirably demonstrated will be our own legacy today to the honour and glory of His name!

---

[26] Derek Prince, *Faith to Live By*, Fort Lauderdale, FL: Derek Prince Ministries, 1977, p. 30.

# Malawi Assemblies of God 2020 Vision

## Presented and Adopted on 16th JULY 2010 by the 2010 General Assembly

## DEVELOPING MALAWI ASSEMBLIES OF GOD (MAG)RE-ALIGNMENT VISION

- **MISSION:** Making Jesus known to everyone everywhere in the power of the Holy Spirit.
- **VISION:** Making missions the driving force of every local church.
- **Habakkuk 2:2** "Write the vision, and make it plain on the tablets, that he who reads it may run."

### MAG Major Goals by 2020

1. 5,000 organized churches by 2020.
   i. 100 Mega churches—from 1,000 processed members each.
   ii. 4,900 churches with an average of 400 processed members in each.
2. 6,000 Trained Ministers: Leadership Development.
3. 2 Million Processed Members all baptized in the Holy Spirit, which then is a tithe of the Malawi population by projection.

### A. Numerical Church Growth

- GOAL: 2 Million Members; a tithe of the population of Malawi by 2020
- Present status by approximation:
  - ❖ 150,000 Members
  - ❖ 1,200 Pastors
  - ❖ 2,000 Churches.

## ➢ What Do We DO?

1.  Massive Crusades and Open Air Campaigns
    i.   Local Church
    ii.  Sections, Districts & Divisions
    iii. National

2.  Strategic Church Planting Campaigns
    i.   Each local church plants a church every year and helps to develop at least two organized churches in the decade.
    ii.  Each local church should send at least three emerging pastors to Bible School.
    iii. Sections, Districts, Divisions & Division of Evangelism and Missions to identify strategic places for church planting and oversee that work commences in all such locations
    iv.  DEM to plant 50 churches in the Decade
    v.   Missionary Partners to plant 10 churches in the Decade

3.  Children and Youth Focus
    i.   Revamping children ministries and youth ministries
    ii.  One Hope, Royal Rangers, Chi-Alpha, etc. to be emphasized

4.  Develop Massive Outreach (Soul Winning) Materials
    i.    Hand Bills
    ii.   Flyers
    iii.  Placards
    iv.   Literature Tracts
    v.    Discipleship Materials
    vi.   Billboards
    vii.  Puppets
    viii. Media Outreach (TV, Radio, Internet, Newspapers & etc)

5.  Enforce Home Cells Church System
    i.   Develop Seminar Materials

    ii.    Conduct Seminars in Sections

6.    Empowerment Training at all Levels of MAG Structure

    i.    Discipleship
    ii.    Follow Up
    iii.    Membership
    iv.    Home Cells Based Church
    v.    Church Administration and Leadership
    vi.    Stewardship (Financial Management)

7.    Strategic Leadership Development

    i.    Train 4,800 Emerging Ministers (To have 6,000 Spirit Filled Leaders)
    ii.    Refresher Leadership Training Programmes
    iii.    Pastoral Refresher Training
    iv.    Targeted NBA and NEC Management Training
    v.    Increasing Intake of AGST, ANTS & AGXS (AGXS to also increase centres)
    vi.    AGXS to operate fully fledged and include divisional one month residential classes
    vii.    Develop three Lay Training Centers
    viii.    Establish MAG University
        a.    AGST, GU & ANTS to merge
        b.    To include at least three constituencies
        c.    To offer Theology and Liberal Arts programmes
        d.    To offer Certificates, Diplomas, BAs, MAs and PhDs

## B. INFRASTRUCTURE GROWTH

    a.    Envisioning 5,000 organized churches
    b.    Official classification of Local Assemblies
    c.    Every District to have 100 complete church buildings of at least 10m x 16m. Central District churches to be at least 15m x 27m.
    d.    Cities to have at least 100 church buildings of 18m x 25m.

e.  100 Mega Churches across the nation: building size of at least 25m x 30m.
f.  Take an inventory of existing structures and call for specified standards of their upkeep.
g.  Acquire Strategic Church Plots and seek deeds for all church properties.
h.  Establishing Office buildings in Blantyre, Lilongwe, Mzuzu and Zomba.
i.  Each Division to have a MAG office
j.  Build National Headquarters
k.  Expand real estate properties
l.  Establish National Broadcasting Station: Radio and Television
m.  Establish Media Office
n.  Establish a Hospital# one or more ?#
o.  Establish Academic Institutions of Lower and Higher Learning
p.  Establish MAG (Lakeside) Cottage
q.  Every district to own a vehicle and motor-bike
r.  100 Mega churches (of at Least 25m x 30m)
   i.   Identify potential mega-churches
   ii.  Empower such churches for mega-church phenomena
   iii. In advance, build infrastructure for mega-church

## C. CHURCH GROWTH

1.  Pentecostal Emphasis (Decade of Pentecost)
   i.    Organizing National Holy Spirit Launch
   ii.   Regional Holy Spirit Convocations
   iii.  One Sunday of every month be Holy Spirit Emphasis Sunday
   iv.   2011 District councils to embrace Holy Spirit theme
   v.    2011 theme of the year be Holy Spirit Emphasis
   vi.   Decade of Pentecost Task Force
   vii.  Annual Pentecostal celebrations (Pentecost Week/Sunday)

viii.    Pentecost must be emphasized throughout in sections, districts, divisions and all national events.

2.    Spiritual Growth
   a.  Prayer Mobilization
   b.  Sunday School Emphasis
   c.  Sunday School Materials Development
   d.  Membership Materials Development
   e.  Home Cells Emphasis

3.    Vision Casting Campaigns
   i.    NBA & NEC to visit all districts
   ii.   Utilize district councils
   iii.  Use every opportune forum
   iv.  Use of printing media (Bible markers, brochures, banners, T/Shirts, etc)

4.    Resource Mobilization
   i.    Empowering Human esource
   ii.   Finance Management System
   iii.  Streamlining and expanding investment base

5.    Establishing Research and Development Council
   i.    Establish its own office/equipment
   ii.   Specialized Human Resource

6.    Utilization and Maximizing Use of ICT
   i.    HQ computerization
   ii.   HQ online system with division offices
   iii.  Website development
   iv.  NBA & NEC be on personal Internet service
   v.   Adopt modern communication facilities
   vi.  ICT training for all pastors

## D. MISSIONARIES' DEPLOYMENT

**Incoming Foreign Missionaries:** Based on the Memorandum of Understanding.

1. Should have specified assignments.
2. Should be resident across the country depending on the assignments.
3. Should contribute towards the national budget every year, as stipulated from time to time.
4. Should be giving a bi-annual comprehensive report of their ministry to NBA.
5. Should be evaluated by the national office.
6. Lobbying; missionaries to sell assets (eg., vehicles) within MAG when changing fields.

### Outgoing National Missionaries

1. Should have a specified task in the field.
2. National office to have an input in choosing candidates.
3. DEM is the sole sending agency and the official authority of all types of missionaries (ie; tent making, bi-vocational and secondment missionaries).
4. All missionaries should abide by DEM policy

## E. HOW THIS WILL BE DONE?

- ✓ Targeted Implementation
- ✓ There be strict monitoring systems to help with the implementation of the vision
- ✓ Special organizing, leading, controlling, directing and funding

# MALAWI ASSEMBLIES OF GOD VISION CAST

## 5 000 CHURCHES BY 2020

### THE MATHEMATICS ON MAG VISION:
- 5,000 churches by 2020
- 400 church members average size
- 6,000 trained pastors by 2020
- equals 2,000,000 members plus, plus

### "HOW CAN THIS BE?"

MATHS CALCULATION:
- Just if every existing church and
- Every church planted now ...
- Plants another church...
- **Every 24 months...**
- *WE WILL BEAT THE TARGET*

*This Means: Every Church Existing Today Will Plant 3 Churches by the End of 2020*

COUNT THE COST: *WHAT COSTS MORE?*
- The cost of working according to God's vision? **or...**
- The cost of working **without** God's vision?
- **Working without vision <u>always costs more</u>**
- **Let's go for it!**
- Let's spend ten more months casting the vision.

HOW THIS WILL HAPPEN:
- Get a clear *vision* by regularly *praying* together
- Mobilize and direct resources only to the **vision**
- **Habakkuk 2:2** "Write the vision, and make it plain on the tablets, that he who reads it may run."

REMEMBER
- No prayer: No Vision!
- No vision: Scattered Resources!
- Scattered Resources: Limited Progress!

RESOURCES TO MOBILIZE:
- **SPIRITUAL** (Regular Prayer Together)
- **HUMAN** (Need 6,000 Pastors)
- **PHYSICAL** (Plots, Buildings, Finances, etc.)

THE VISION MUST BE KNOWN AND OWNED BY:
- Every Individual MAG Member,
- Every MAG Pastor,
- Every MAG Section Presbyter,
- Every District Leader,
- Every Division Leader,
- Every MAG Missionary,
- Every National Executive Member
- Every National Board of Administration
- Every Outside Supporter/Missions Partners

**THE VISION *MUST BE CONTINUOUSLY KEPT BEFORE THE PEOPLE***

PRAYER MUST BE:
- With Purpose
- With Priority
- With Proper Plan
- With Full Participation

***GOD IS DOING SOMETHING IN MALAWI AND HE WANTS TO INCLUDE ALL OF US.***

We are all Members of the same Team:
- Individuals
- Pastors
- Missionaries
- Section, District and Division Leaders

- General Assembly Officers

Each One of us Must be Ready to Answer the Question:

*What Would I Do ...?*
- If God calls me to become like Christ in every way?
- If God calls me to serve the church or plant a church?
- If many individuals from my congregation each desire to **plant** a church?
- If God raises up many people who want to **serve** within the church?
- If someone wants to plant a local assembly within the same area I am?

Each General Presbytery Member and Missionary Must Have an Answer to this Big Question:

## WHAT IS THE VISION OF THE MALAWI ASSEMBLIES OF GOD?

We Must All Answer:
- What will I do with the vision God has given us?
- What will I do when the vision starts to be fulfilled?
- What will I do when the vision seems to be dying?

National Leaders and Missionaries Must Answer:
- How are we to respond knowing that MAG General Assembly said "yes!" to the great vision for the church?
- How are we to respond if every local assembly has a prospective candidate for theological training in line with the great vision for MAG?
- How will 3,000 church pastors/planters be trained in the next six years?

**Meditate on This**

**If Not Now, WHEN? ... If Not Here, WHERE? ... If Not Us, WHO? ... If Not This Way? ... HOW THEN?**

### 5,000 by 2020!
~~~~~~~~~~~~~~~~~~~~

## REFERENCE LIST

Adeyemo, Tokunbo, "Leadership" in the *Africa Bible Commentary*, Nairobi: WordAlive, 2006.

Barna, George, *Think Like Jesus*, Nashville, Thomas Nelson, 2003.

Berkhof, Louis, *A Summary of Christian Doctrine*, Edinburgh: Banner of Truth Trust, 2005.

Brown, George W., *The Fruit of the Spirit,* Grantham: Stanborough Press, 1998.

Eims, Leroy. "The Lost Art of Disciple Making" in *Readings and Resource Materials for Developing a Christian Worldview,* Springfield, MI: Global University, 2005.

Elliston, Edgar J., *Home Grown Leaders*, Pasadena: William Carey Library, 1992.

Ferguson, Sinclair B., *The Christian Life,* Edinburgh: Banner of Truth Trust, 1989.

Galgalo, Joseph D,. *African Christianity: The Stranger Within*. Nairobi: Zapf Chancery, 2012.

Hendricks, Howard G. and William D. Hendricks. *Living by the Book: Principles for Christian Living from the Bible to Live By*. Chicago: Moody Press, 1991.

Kuert, William P., "A Study of the Redemptive Change Process from a Biblical and Psychological Perspective" in *Readings and Resource Materials for Developing a Christian Worldview,* Springfield: Global University, 2005.

Lee, Harris W., *Effective Church Leadership: A Practical Sourcebook*. Silver Springs, MD: Ministerial Association, GCSDA, 2003.

O'Donovan, Wilbur, *Biblical Christianity in African Perspective.* Carlisle, UK: Paternoster Press, 1996.

Ortberg, John, "The Last Taboo," *Leadership Journal*, Vol. XV No. 2, 1994.

Packer, J.I., *Evangelism and the Sovereignty of God*, Downers Grove, IL: InterVarsity Press, 1961.

Packer, J.I., *Knowing God*, Downers Grove, IL: InterVarsity Press, 1973.

Prince, Derek, *Faith to Live By*, Fort Lauderdale, FL: Derek Prince Ministries, 1977.

Stein, Robert H., *A Basic Guide to Interpreting the Bible*. Grand Rapids, MI: Baker Academic, 1994.

Wadge, Judy, *Be a Winner: Principles of Spiritual Warfare*, Nairobi: Life Challenge Africa, 2006.

West, Robert M., *How to Study the Bible*, Ulrichsville, OH: Barbour Publishing, 2007.

Printed in the United States
By Bookmasters